What's Up
with Worship?

What's Up
with Worship?

Gary McBride

WHAT'S UP WITH WORSHIP?
By: Gary McBride
Copyright © 2013
GOSPEL FOLIO PRESS
All Rights Reserved

Published by
GOSPEL FOLIO PRESS
304 Killaly St. W.
Port Colborne, ON L3K 6A6
CANADA

ISBN: 9781927521359

Cover design by Danielle Elzinga

All Scripture quotations from the
King James Version unless otherwise noted.

Printed in USA

FOREWARD

I have known Gary McBride for over thirty years. We have spent times of worship together breaking bread with other believers and we have enjoyed times of quiet communion together, discussing the things of God and more particularly the wonders, the glories and the person of Christ.

These times constitute precious memories for me and they remain foundational in many ways to my understanding and appreciation of what worship is all about.

Gary has practised in both the corporate and personal context the worship which he preaches in this book. He is not so much concerned with the external and the liturgical, the mechanical and the formulaic except to warn as to the pitfalls and traps that undue reliance upon these things can present.

That is not to say that God is unconcerned as to how in the organizational sense we should approach Him—far from it. But the principles and precepts of scripture have more to do with the attitude of the worshiper's heart than they do with his/her actions in worship. This is what Gary's book is all about—as is his life.

Ralph Carr
Timmins, Ontario

PREFACE

The following collection of thoughts comes from a concern for the loss of what should be central in assembly life. As the title suggests, the issue at hand is worship.

I have spent my entire life in "the assemblies" and have invested time and effort seeking to edify and encourage God's people. In the course of my ministry I have been intimately involved in a dozen assemblies. In travels, I have visited at least thirty assemblies in various parts of the world. In North America, I have been in more than sixty assemblies. Out of these experiences I have enjoyed many "remembrance meetings," with the Lord's people.

One of the hallmarks of assembly life is that the breaking of bread is accompanied by a time of corporate worship. It is not just the act of "remembering the Lord," in the bread and cup but gathering for worship that is distinctive. Nearly all believers, world-wide and in all types of gatherings, "remember Him" as the Lord Jesus has requested. What is missing in most local churches is a dedicated time for corporate worship that allows men the opportunity to lead the Lord's people in worship.

The purpose of this book is to challenge the thinking of God's people. As you read *What's Up With Worship*, please search the Scriptures to see if these things are so. Some of what is written in "concrete" in assembly life is not written in the Bible. Practices can and have been developed from inferences, from traditions and even from the silences of Scripture.

My concern is that worship is in decline; this is true even where there is a dedicated time of worship. Men in particular are not investing time and energy into the study of God's word and are not enjoying times of fellowship with their Lord. This is having an effect on the worship meeting—especially the quality of verbal expression.

I enjoy assembly life, and am in fellowship in a local church that has worship as part of the observance of the Lord's Supper.

·

What's Up With Worship?

My conviction is that worship is to be central to the life of the assembly and of the individual. For this reason I choose to meet as I do, and am committed to this type of gathering.

This book is written out of concern: concern for local assemblies and also for God's glory. My prayer is that God would bless this work for the good of His people and for His glory.

> To Calvary, Lord, in spirit now our grateful souls repair,
> To dwell upon Thy dying love, and taste its sweetness there.
> Sweet resting-place of every heart that feels the plague of sin,
> Yet knows the deep mysterious joy of peace with God within.
>
> E. Denny

CONTENTS

ACKNOWLEDGEMENTS

Many of the thoughts expressed in *"What's Up With Worship"* are a result of the influence and teaching of others over many years. There are no footnotes nor is there a bibliography as it would be impossible to give all the credits that are due.

In the production of this manuscript I am thankful for the input and suggestions of David Reed, (St. Catharines). His feedback helped me to organize and formulate the thoughts. I am also grateful to David and Lynn Shatford, (Pelham) for their efforts in editing the manuscript. I appreciate Ralph Carr (Timmins) penning the forward and am thankful for his encouragement over many years. Sam Cairns of Gospel Folio Press has a part as well in this coming to print and I thank him and the staff at GFP. I am also thankful to my wife, Gloria, for her input, questions, suggestions and encouragement on this topic that means so much to both of us.

Most of all I am thankful to the Lord for my heritage. My mother was brought to the Lord by a school friend and came into assembly fellowship in the north of England. Years later the Lord directed her steps and she found an assembly in Toronto and there I was raised. I can say with the Psalmist, *"The lines have fallen to me in pleasant places; Yes, I have a good inheritance"* (Ps. 16:6).

chapter one

THE LORD'S SUPPER AND WORSHIP

There is great divide in the Church, the Body of Christ, which likely comes as no surprise to most believers. This divide I am talking about is not a matter of doctrine or even biblical interpretation, but rather of practice. There must be a warning given at this point—practice does not produce spirituality. In fact, certain customs that are unique to any group may become a source of pride, and thus lead to a sinful attitude.

The practice that is seen in some local churches and not in others is the weekly observance of the Lord's Supper accompanied by a time of worship. The "breaking of bread" can occur apart from a specified time of worship. In most denominational churches, its observance follows either ministry or a gospel message. The Lord is still remembered and believers are obedient to the command to "remember Him".

On the other hand, worship can take place at times separate from the "breaking of bread". Believers can worship on their own or gather with other saints and worship in their homes, at a camp site or in other venues. Worship is not reserved for one hour per week nor is it the exclusive property of a certain group. Regardless of how individual believers meet, worship should be part of every Christian's life.

What is Common

This is not a matter of spirituality, as those who observe the Lord's Supper with a different frequency and in a different manner may be spiritual. In fact, they may well be more spiritual than those who observe the Lord's Supper weekly. Spirituality is a result of growth, devotion and obedience and no practice can produce these qualities. Spiritual maturity is a matter of growing into the likeness of Christ, and as such is purely between an individual and the Lord Jesus.

In evangelical circles, the Lord's Supper, or Communion as it is sometimes called, is considered to be a fundamental part of church life. Most evangelicals would view the Lord's Supper and believer's baptism as ordinances—exclusively the only two given to the Church. They would, for the most part, view baptism as a once-for-all act speaking of our death with Christ. The Lord's Supper is seen as an ongoing expression of the Lord's death for us.

There is no doubt about the institution and purpose of the Lord's Supper. It was instituted by the Lord Jesus the night in which He was betrayed (Luke 22:14-20). The desire of His heart was to eat the Passover meal with His disciples, and in the process, He took two of the elements of that supper—the bread and the cup and instituted something new: the Lord's Supper. The purpose was that this would be repeated as an act of devotion done in remembrance of Him.

It is obvious from the book of Acts that the early church in Jerusalem did practice or observe this command of the Lord. Acts 2:42 lists four activities of the early believers: teaching, praying, fellowship and the breaking of bread. All four of these are endorsed in the epistles as fundamental to church life.

In Acts 2:46 the early believers broke bread from house to house, which may simply refer to sharing a meal together. However, the language does not exclude the possibility that they were *"remembering the Lord"*.

In Acts 20:7, Paul was at Troas and the disciples *"came together to break bread"*. This is usually taken to mean that this was the regular custom. This conclusion is by way of inference rather than by revelation. The context reveals nothing as to how these believers functioned and what they did, other than that Paul preached to them and they observed the Lord's Supper. These references in Acts are the sum of the historical basis in Scripture for the observance of the Lord's Supper.

The other scriptural clue about the day of the week that believers gathered is found in 1 Corinthians 16:2 regarding bringing an offering on the first day of the week. The use of the phrase *"the Lord's day"* in Revelation 1 has wonderful devotional implications but does not prove anything with regard to corporate life.

What is Unknown

Within the Christian world, there is much variety as to how the "ordinance" of the Lord's Supper is conducted, and how often it is observed. When Scripture is studied objectively and with sound methods of interpretation, it is clear that there is very little teaching about the Lord's Supper. In particular there is no revelation as to how it was done as to practice and procedure, nothing about format or frequency, or whether it was a separate assembly or an exercise that was part of another local church.

There is no pattern to follow as to what accompanied the "breaking of bread and the drinking of the cup". The Lord and the disciples sang one hymn in the upper room after the supper. That is the only reference to singing that accompanied the observance of the Lord's Supper. Prior to taking the bread and cup the Lord Jesus was engaged in a teaching session as recorded in John 13 and 14. In Acts 20, Paul preached, but the content of the message is not known. Before passing the bread and the cup, the Lord Jesus prayed and gave thanks. This is the only mention of prayer in connection to the "Lord's Supper". There is little evidence from the Gospels or the book of the Acts to build a case on how to observe the "Lord's Supper".

As to some of the issues previously mentioned, Scripture is silent with regard to almost all of church life. There is virtually no instruction as to how things are to be done. Nothing is said about how often to meet, the time or length, the format or flow of the "assembly". There is no teaching about corporate singing or music, hymn books or choruses. There is nothing about what children are to do during meeting times, or how believers are to dress, nothing about where they are to sit nor if and when they were to stand.

Some Christians have selectively built doctrine out of the silence of Scripture or a phrase taken out of context. Verses, or a text, taken out of context become a pretext for how things ought to be done. For instance policies on dress have been taken from Peter's action in John 21 of putting on his coat before he went to see the Lord. The silence of Scripture on musical instruments is used to reinforce a stand on music but the fact that the Bible does not mention hymn books is overlooked. That Paul stayed in Troas until the Sunday and the disciples came together to "break bread" is sometime presented as proof that there is only one day of the week to observe "the breaking of bread".

Quite likely based on the institution of the Lord's Supper in the upper room and the time the saints gathered in Troas, the "breaking of bread" was in the evening. Traditionally and historically it has been observed on a Sunday but even for this issue there is no "thus says the Lord". Here again, there is no definitive word to say that this should be the standard practice for all time and in all places.

What is Different

Among those who gather weekly to remember the Lord and who are generally known by others as "Brethren," there is some conformity to a pattern. What is unique, or has been historically, is a dedicated time of worship surrounding the "breaking of bread". The particular pattern in an assembly usually conforms to what was introduced when the assembly was established. In this way, assemblies around the world may have similarities in the way they meet, but there can also be differences. The distinctions are likely due to the background of the original evangelist and where he came from in the first place.

There are usually some practices that are unique to assemblies in other countries. For instance, in India many believers will kneel on the floor as a brother gives thanks for the bread and cup. In some Eastern European countries, the saints stand while a brother prays but they would likely never stand to sing a hymn. Some meetings will have portions of Scripture shared during the meeting, while there are others where it is worship only in prayer and the singing of hymns.

Even the emblems that are used cover an array of ingredients and styles. In some places a single cup is used; though usually when the meeting is larger, multiple "single cups" are utilized. Other assemblies use individual cups or some combination of single and multiple cups. The contents of the "cup" may vary from wine to grape juice, and in some countries, juice or cola. The bread might be leavened or unleavened, and again in some countries, it might be crackers or cookies. There are meetings that use a cloth to cover the bread and cup after they have been passed, while others have no such custom. Here again in all these matters the Scriptures give no definitive word from the Lord. Believers develop practices and perhaps convictions based on inferences and preferences.

The format may differ from country to country or from culture to culture. The size of the fellowship may have an effect on how things are arranged. In some places the Christians gather in a circle, some gather in a square, and others sit in rows with a table at the front. There are assemblies where the men sit on one side and women on the other, and some where the men sit at the front around the table while the women sit in rows looking on. There are meetings that use a musical instrument to help with the singing, while others would prefer not to do so.

Some saints feel very strongly about any number of these issues. People have left meetings over the issue of one cup or many cups, the use of wine or grape juice, or leavened versus unleavened bread. The issue of musical accompaniment is a major item to many people and would be grounds to avoid a place or leave for another meeting. Even whether there should be a cloth or napkin as a cover has been hotly contested in places. People may have strong opinions about the arrangement of the chairs while forgetting that the early believers had no chairs at all.

What is Unique

In light of the above, the question may well be asked, "What difference would it make as to how and when the Lord's Supper is observed?" Does it matter if the "breaking of bread" is observed at the end of a ministry meeting or is there value in incorporating a time of corporate worship? The answer is not necessarily found explicitly stated in Scripture but rather in principle.

The divide in evangelicalism is this: either worship is the center or focal point of assembly life or the platform is central. Specifying a regular time of worship allows worship, at least potentially, to become central to assembly life and practice. The life of the assembly would focus on worship as the central facet of corporate life. The alternative is that the platform and preaching become the center of church life.

An assembly is only worship-centered to the extent that there is worship. The format of the meeting does not guarantee that worship will result. In the same way, a local church that has as its center the platform and a spiritual man in it, may be Christ centered and worshipful. The point is this: the format does not guarantee the result.

The fact of having a dedicated time for worship does not insure that worship will actually take place. In some assemblies, little or no worship takes place. There may be the singing of hymns, reading of the Word, and praying, but all with no concept of what worship entails. What does take place may well be man-centered, merely the sharing of good things that have happened to us during the week. It could also be a matter of rote, where the same men say the same things, pray the same prayers, and give out the same hymns week after week. In this way the meeting becomes mechanical and departs from the realm of spiritual exercise.

Where there is appreciation of the person of Jesus Christ, adoration is expressed to the Father about the Son, then where true worship takes place. The saints fulfill the words of the Lord Jesus about worshiping in spirit and truth, out of hearts full of Him. This is the basis for worship becoming the center of assembly life and practice.

The present age is different than any previous era, in that our society is so mobile. Families move for a variety of reasons — perhaps most often for economic reasons related to a job and income. There is little allegiance to institutions; people change banks, doctors, jobs and environments in ways never seen in more static societies. This is true, as well, in church life. People will move from one local church to another based perhaps on preference and convenience. Conviction is not always at the top of the list of reasons when choosing where to fellowship.

Often people leave assemblies for another style of meeting without thinking about the following principle: either worship or the platform is the center of church life. The choice is between a place where the pulpit is the focal point or one where worship is at its center. In fairness, people may have been in an assembly where there was no real worship, and so they have not seen worship function as the center of church life. The act of leaving, however, will in all likelihood rob them of the opportunity to see a worship-centered local church in action. This should be a matter of serious and sober thought.

There are also people who major on the minors. They make important matters out of issues where Scripture is silent. Sometimes, and in some places, these things can lead to a lack of peace and an atmosphere of contention. Often, when this occurs, the purpose of the worship meeting — the focus on the Lord Jesus — is lost. If this type of thing happens, people who profess to love Christ end up putting the pattern ahead of His person. The irony is that while holding to the importance of worship, the atmosphere can become so tense (or even toxic) that no worship can possibly occur.

If, as many profess, worship is the principle thing, it is good to focus on how worship takes place. It is also worthwhile to explore the ingredients and importance of worship, and to consider, as A. W. Tozer said, that in church-life and practice, "Worship was the missing jewel".

What's Up With Worship?

Lord Jesus Christ, our Saviour Thou,
  With joy we worship Thee,
We know Thou hast redeemest us,
  by dying on the tree.
Our theme of praise art Thou alone—
  Thy cross, Thy work, Thy Word.
Oh, who can fathom all Thy love,
  Thou living blessed Lord?

Author Unknown

chapter two

THE PRINCIPLE OF WORSHIP

Life in a local church might be so much simpler if the Lord had given minute directions as to how to meet and function. It may be easy to think this because church life seems to be wide open as to procedure. The Lord gave very specific instructions to Israel in the Old Testament as to how they would camp, travel, worship, and approach God. Very little, if any thing in the spiritual life of Israel was left to the whims and wishes of men.

However, the New Testament is virtually silent on organization—that is, how things are to be done regarding worship. There is some instruction in 1 Corinthians 14 about meetings with the general instruction that all things are to be done in order. Some believers pick up on that statement and make rules based on what they think decency and order implies. The very act of doing so may go beyond what Scripture would say on the matter.

Over the years there have been brethren who would appeal to Old Testament practices and apply these to church life, while at the same time they would teach against structured churches with practices rooted in the Old Testament and against legalism. They would themselves develop procedures based on directives given to Israel and out of narrative passages. For example, teaching on the Tabernacle, or Nehemiah's walls has been used to formulate New Testament practice.

The tradition in what are known as "brethren assemblies" is to have a dedicated meeting for observing the Lord's Supper, which involves worship. For this reason the phrase, "worship meeting" is often used although it does not occur in Scripture. It is this "worship meeting" that is the distinctive feature of assembly life, as believers in most denominational churches would observe the "Lord's Supper".

Experientially, there are two common complaints from those who have left assemblies for a different type or style of local church. One complaint relates to the infrequency of observing the Lord's Supper in a denominational church. The other has to do with the lack of a dedicated time of corporate worship. Ironically for many who come from denominations to assemblies, these are among the very things they find attractive about assembly life.

Often the sign outside of a denominational church will designate the Sunday morning meeting as a time of worship or a "worship meeting". This is the designation whether it is a gospel or ministry meeting. In most evangelical churches worship is associated with the music in the opening of the meeting. Worship may indeed take place in the hearts of individuals and depending on the group, it may happen corporately as well. It must be remembered that in assemblies, a hymn book and singing is used as part of the time of worship at the Lord's Supper. But, what is missing in these other formats is the participation of various men in the verbal expression of worship.

There is, generally speaking, a lack of understanding as to what worship is and how it is expressed. This is true in the broader evangelical church as well as in assemblies. The fact of having a "worship meeting" is no guarantee that worship is understood or even that it takes place. There are assemblies where believers come together week after week to "remember the Lord" at the "worship meeting," and yet worship rarely, if ever, happens.

What is Worship

In the Old Testament, the word "worship", according to *Strong's Hebrew Dictionary* means "to prostrate, to bow down, to stoop, or to give obeisance". The first mention of this Hebrew word in Scripture is of Abraham in Genesis 18:2—he *"bowed himself to the ground"*. The second mention is in Genesis 22:5

where Abraham said, *"The lad and I will go yonder and worship"*. These two occurrences of the word are fitting introductions to what worship entails. It involves both a humble attitude and an offering up of acceptable sacrifices to God.

Outside of the book of Psalms, worship is often non verbal but is expressed by a person falling on his face after a revelation of God's glory. Worship was also seen in the sacrifice of a burnt offering by a pious Israelite. This was a voluntary sweet-savor offering and was wholly consumed to speak of the fact that it was given to God. Throughout the Old Testament, obeisance (bowing down) and offering (sending up) were the elements of worship.

To these two could be added verbal expressions such as are found in the Psalms. For example, Psalm 72:19 *"And blessed be His glorious name forever, and let the whole earth be filled with His glory. Amen and Amen"*. Another among many is found in Psalm 96:7-9 *"Give to the LORD, O kindreds of the peoples, Give to the LORD, glory and strength. Give to the LORD the glory due His name: bring an offering and come into His courts. O worship the LORD in the beauty of holiness! Tremble before Him all the earth"*. In these verses the offering is verbal, not visual. The offerer comes in humility and offers up words of worship to God.

In the New Testament according to *Vine's Expository Dictionary* there are five Greek verbs translated by the English word "worship". These words have to do with either an act or an attitude. They include the ideas of "reverence, homage, awe, devotion, to honour, or even service".

Vine says this of worship: "The worship of God is nowhere defined in Scripture. A consideration of the above verbs shows that it is not confined to praise; broadly it may be regarded as the direct acknowledgement of God, of His nature, attributes, ways and claims, whether by the outgoing of the heart in praise and thanksgiving or by deed done in such acknowledgement".

Warren Wiersbe has defined worship as "the believer's response of all that he is—mind, emotions, will, and body—to all that God is and says and does".

Someone else has defined it this way: "Worship is the total adoring response of man to the eternal God and as such it is to be personal and passionate".

The first mention of worship in the New Testament is in the story of the Wise Men in Matthew 2. They came with the express purpose of worshiping the King of the Jews and when they found Him, worshiped by falling down and giving gifts. It has been well said, that "Wise Men still seek Him".

The conversation between the Lord Jesus and the woman of Samaria in John 4 is vital to the understanding of worship. The Lord Jesus leads this woman in her understanding, teaching her that worship is not confined to a place, but is rather about "a person." He reveals to her and to us that worship can be true or it can be false. It can be done in ignorance, or it can be done in knowledge of the one who is being worshiped. It can be an act of the flesh or it can be a spiritual activity. Of course, only what is done in "spirit and truth" qualifies as real worship and is acceptable to God.

Worship that is "in spirit and truth" goes beyond ritual, and conforms to the Word of God. The Jews engaged in ritual while the Samaritans worshiped what they did not know. For us the application is that worship must come from within. It is a spiritual activity where our spirit responds to God. This takes worship out of the realm of the flesh, making it an activity that cannot be manufactured by man. Worship must also be in line with God's Word. His Word is truth, and so there must be reality based on God's revelation.

What is not Worship

In some places, there is an effort to manufacture or produce worship through a change in the format or structure of the "worship meeting". This may be a response to prolonged silences and lack of participation in the meeting. The motivation for change often develops from the fact that few men participate. The times of silence are so long and obvious that they become embarrassing, and the result is that people conclude "something should be done".

The effort to fix this usually results in changes that may produce participation and that likely do remove the silences; but no more worship occurs than it previously did. The meetings generally become a sharing of experiences that touched the life during the past week. These may be good things and are evidence of God's hand at work, but they focus on what has happened to us. As such, the meeting can become "man-centered" instead of "Christ-centered".

Some have suffered through these times of spiritual poverty and for this reason have tried to innovate through change. Perhaps, based on their view of the issue, they have allowed women to participate verbally to various extents. The spiritual condition of the women is not usually the problem, because in most places the women do worship, though in silence. Other than a change in conviction on the issue of "women's participation," it is most likely a response to the poor spiritual state of the men. The fact that men do not offer up worship and do not take leadership creates a vacuum that will be filled in some other way.

There are also assemblies that experience a decline in attendance at the Lord's Supper, where the Lord's people have little or no concern or commitment. Various means have been adopted to try to solve this issue. The act of "breaking bread" may be added to another meeting, that is, there is no longer a dedicated time of worship. Again, it needs to be reiterated that Scripture nowhere says this is wrong or even unspiritual. It is a pragmatic way of solving a problem; but it removes worship as the center of church life.

Even in assemblies where there is a dedicated "worship meeting", there is no guarantee that worship will or does take place. Using the phrase "worship meeting" does not produce worship. Worship is an activity of the heart that is taken up with Christ. Even in meetings where lack of participation is not the issue, true worship may not take place.

Thoughts about Worship

Many believers do not understand the distinctions between thanksgiving, praise and worship. As a result there can be giving of thanks and praise to God but an absence of worship. Thanksgiving is a proper and fitting response to what has been done for us and given to us. Praise is that which is offered up to the one who has done the giving.

Worship involves both thanksgiving and praise and these two elements are an integral part of worship. Worship, however, goes beyond these activities to occupation with the person of God the Father or of the Lord Jesus Christ, that is, to be occupied with Christ because we love Him and quite apart from what He has done for us and what has been received by us.

An illustration given in the oral ministry by the late Dan Snaddon has always stuck with me and is worth sharing. If you are invited to someone's home and receive a meal, you will say thank-you. It is fitting to respond to what has been done for you and is only good manners. If the meal has been particularly good or the effort put in has gone above what is normally experienced, you may go beyond thanks and you may praise your host or hostess. Regardless of the quality of the meal you are unlikely to offer worship—that is, to bow down and proclaim how great they are quite apart from what you got out of the whole experience.

This is applicable to the spiritual realm. Thanksgiving and praise are both functionally part of the expression of worship. Worship will flow from a thankful heart; thanksgiving is the appreciation of what has been received by us. Praise is to be the natural response of the believer to all that the Lord has done. Worship, however, goes beyond thanksgiving and praise, and is the occupation of the saints with the person of Christ. It is here another great divide takes place in that some Christians never go beyond thanksgiving and praise to worship. They have never known what it is to be lost in adoring wonder, losing sight of self, and being totally taken up with the Saviour, the Lord Jesus Christ.

How to Promote Worship

The question may be asked, "What is the solution to the issues raised above? Is there a way to resolve the poverty of silence and the absence of true worship?" The answer is in the heart of the individual, perhaps more so the men than the women, and has to do with how time is spent during the week. The next chapter deals with the root of the matter—that is, where worship comes from.

> Lord Jesus, we worship and bow at Thy feet,
> And give Thee the glory, the honour that's meet.
> While through Thee, O Saviour our praises ascend
> And join in the chorus that never shall end.
>
> Author Unknown

chapter three

THE LORD'S TABLE AND WORSHIP

There is generally little understanding of the distinctions between the Lord's Table and the Lord's Supper. Not only are they separate phrases, but the teaching given regarding each is different. Failure to understand the Lord's Table is at the root of many of the issues that relate to worship. This is especially true when the Lord's Supper is attached to a time of worship.

Teaching on both the Table and the Supper, is presented in 1 Corinthians. The Lord's Table is found in 10:14-22 while the instruction regarding the Lord's Supper is in 11:17-34. Interpretation of these two passages is often merged because both include the bread and the cup. Out of this confusion some extra-biblical terminology has been applied to the "worship meeting." Phrases such as "protecting the table", or "guarding the table", and even "a table of convenience". The problem with these phrases, when misapplied, is that they substantiate unbiblical practices and concepts.

What is Different

The starting place for interpretation is exegesis, that is, to determine the meaning of the words, the sentence, and the flow of thought. Key to this process is the understanding of the context—first of the book, and next of the immediate passage. As has been said, a text out of context becomes a pretext for a particular point of view or practice.

The context of 1 Corinthians is that in chapters 1-6 Paul deals with the matters in the assembly he had heard about from Chloe's household. These were issues that were causing quarrels (1:11).

What's Up With Worship?

Starting in chapter 7:1, Paul answers questions that the believers had asked in a letter. The questions had to do with marriage, food offered to idols, order in the assembly, and the resurrection. The passage about the Lord's Table falls in the section that deals with food offered to idols and Christian liberty (chapters 8-10).

Though the letter is a church epistle, and thus intended for the whole gathering, the instruction in this section must be heeded by individuals. This teaching has to do with the exercise of a person's own liberty regarding food offered to idols in light of the conscience of others. This is crucial to a proper interpretation of the teaching on the Lord's Table.

The instruction on the Lord's Supper is part of extended teaching about "church order". This includes teaching on the uncovered head of the man and the covered head of the woman. It also deals with the exercise of gifts, the exhibition of love, and the excesses of tongues. The more immediate context, 1 Corinthians 11:18, shows it is a corporate setting, *"when you come together as a church"*. This is also true in verse 20, *"when you come together in one place"*.

There are a number of distinctions between the Table and the Supper that should be noted. In this regard, the following chart may help to highlight some of the differences.

The Lord's Table	The Lord's Supper
Fellowship	Remembrance
Always	As often as
Spread by the Lord	Spread by us
Cup first	Bread first
Communion	Proclamation
Cannot	Must Not

There are other differences but these ones are worthy of consideration. The emphasis for the Table is communion or fellowship. The Lord's Table is the place where believers individually meet the Lord and feed on His provision. The Table in this sense spans time and goes on into eternity. It is not something that can be controlled by others nor dictated by law and custom.

There is an absolute impossibility attached to the Lord's Table that is not true of the Lord's Supper. That is, *"you cannot partake of the Lord's table and the table of demons,"* 1 Corinthians 10: 21. Believers can and often do things during the week that are done in secret; no one knows all that others have done between Sundays. For example, it would be possible to "eat in a pagan temple" on Thursday and show up to break bread on Sunday. It would not be in the realm of the impossible. However it is absolutely impossible to fellowship at a pagan table and fellowship at the Lord's Table. The reason is that the Lord controls His table and He will not commune with a person who puts himself out of fellowship with his Lord.

The basis of communion with the Lord at His table is the cup that He drank. The cup is mentioned first, because it is only through His shed blood that believers have communion with the Lord. As a result of His blood, believers can and do have their sins forgiven, and have been called into fellowship. The bread speaks of the unity of the body of Christ and on that basis Christians have the enjoyment of identification with Christ. They can also feed on Him—that is, experience the intimacy of that communion, to learn from Him and to grow in experiential knowledge of Him.

The unity spoken of in 1 Corinthians 10:17, *"For we being many, are one bread, and one body; for we all partake of that one bread,"* is nowhere seen or experienced in this world. This unity is absolutely true at the Lord's Table, in that fellowship with the Lord Jesus does not depend on all believers being in agreement with each other. There are differences of practice, of interpretation, of standards, and even of doctrine but there is unity at the Lord's Table. No one believer could possibly refuse another believer a place at the Lord's Table as it is a matter solely between the individual and his Lord.

Some brethren feel compelled to "protect the table," but as seen, this is impossible for any man to do. Another common expression used at the Lord's Supper is a word of "welcome to the Lord's Table," or often it may be "as we gather at the Lord's Table." The use of this terminology confuses the issues at hand and blurs the distinctions between the Table and the Supper.

Sitting at His Table

The larger issue in our day and age is that relatively few believers take time to sit at the Lord's Table and commune with Him. There are so many things that occupy the time and the mind, there are so many places to go and our society is highly mobile. Children are involved in activities that demand attention, leaving little time for a devotional life. Entertainment, whether television, the internet, movies or sports are so readily available; but, once again, are time consuming. All of this deprives us of time to sit and commune, to be in the Word, to talk to the Lord, or just to enjoy His Person. This wonderful relationship can easily become one-sided where He loves us and desires fellowship, but where we find ourselves too busy for Him. He is seen, as in Revelation 3:20, on the out- side of the local assembly, knocking, and asking if there is any individual interested in enjoying fellowship with Him.

There is a need to see this modeled; a good example can demonstrate the enjoyment that comes from spending time with the Lord Jesus. Exhortation can highlight the need and encouragement may spur others in this direction. Individuals, however, must be moved by love for the Lord and by His love for them. They must also be willing to submit to the direction of the Holy Spirit before this problem is solved.

This is the root of any problem with the "worship meeting," and as such cannot be remedied by organization. If the Lord's people do not meet with their Lord during the week there will be nothing to offer in worship on a Sunday. Assemblies can make all the changes that can be thought of but not one iota of worship will be produced. The only change that would be effective is the amount of time individuals spend at the Lord's Table.

An illustration of these truths can be found in Deuteronomy 26:1-15. Though it is directed at Israel, there can be lessons for us. In verse 2 the command is given to gather the first fruits and put them in a basket and bring the basket to the place the Lord specifies. There is an acknowledgement in verse 3 that all they have is from the Lord and has been given by Him. In verses 5-7 there is an awareness of what they were—small in number and slaves to the Egyptians. Verses 8 and 9 express the appreciation they felt for what the Lord had done in bringing them out of Egypt and into Canaan. In verse 4 and again in verse 10 there is action, placing the basket before the altar as an act of worship.

These are the ingredients needed today to worship the Lord.

> **Acknowledgement:** that all that is counted as ours comes from the Lord. This is true in the physical and in the spiritual realm. What is given to Him comes from His hand.

> **Awareness:** of what we were and what we have been saved from, the value of our salvation.

> **Appreciation:** for all that the Lord has done and who He is.

> **Action:** bringing worship to the Lord.

A New Testament illustration can be found in the actions of Mary in Mark 14:3-9. Mary brought a bottle of very expensive perfume, broke the bottle and anointed the Lord Jesus. The application for us is that there is preparation and presentation involved, and that the material is costly and precious.

> **Preparation:** the contents could speak of what has been enjoyed of the person of Christ during the week and which is brought in thought to the time of worship.

> **Presentation:** given in worship the fragrance of those things concerning His Son ascends as a sweet-savor to the Father.

I have often thought that these two illustrations could be applied to the time of corporate worship. At the entrance to the meeting place a sign could pose the question, Is your basket full? At the exit the question might be, Is your bottle broken? These questions would certainly alert people to the issues at hand.

A further thought from both of these illustrations is that the size of the basket and the size of the bottle are not specified. A person who is more mature in the Lord or has been saved longer may have a larger "basket" or "bottle", that is, a greater capacity to enjoy the Lord. Along with the greater capacity comes a greater responsibility to fill up with and pour out in worship. To the extent that this happens, the lack of worship will be addressed and the time together will be filled and fragrant.

On Sundays believers gather at the Lord's Supper to remember their Saviour. This is not the Lord's Table that He has set for His own but it is the Supper that His own have set for Him as He commanded. This Supper is where the Lord's people come to remember Him and to show forth His death until He comes again. Worship will be part of that experience if His own people come prepared as a result of spending time at His Table during the week.

There is a cost to sitting at the Lord's Table as it takes discipline and effort. No one can force another to enjoy the Lord but rather this has to flow from a heart of devotion. It is good to remember David's words in 2 Samuel 24:24, *"nor will I offer a burnt offering to the Lord my God which costs me nothing"*. The cost may involve a change of lifestyle, saying no to other things…or even getting out of bed sooner!

> When I survey the wondrous cross, on which the
>   Lord of Glory died,
> My richest gain I count but loss, and pour contempt
>   on all my pride.
>
> Forbid it, Lord, that I should boast, save in the cross
>   of Christ my God,

All the vain things that charm me most—I sacrifice them to His blood.

See from His head, His hands, His feet; sorrow and love flow mingled down.
Did e'er such love and sorrow meet, or thorns compose so rich a crown?

Were the whole realm of nature mine, that were an offering far too small.
Love so amazing, so divine, demands my heart, my life, my all!

Isaac Watts

chapter four

THE PRACTICE OF WORSHIP

Though it is true that worship flows from time spent with the Lord Jesus at His Table, there are aspects of worship that need to be taught and understood. For those who are young in the faith or new to corporate worship there must be some instruction. The thoughts enjoyed during the week have to be expressed in an appropriate manner to be appreciated by others.

The "appropriate manner" does not refer to being somber or serious looking; there is no premium on looking sad. Worship is not limited to a certain terminology or hymns that are from a particular era. Most people have expectations with regard to how things are done, and any variation tends to be disturbing to some in the group. This is often seen if dress standards are not met or if a certain order is not followed.

There is certainly liberty, as nothing is prescribed in regard to a worship meeting. Individual assemblies can choose to be very structured. Conversely an assembly can, in their autonomy, decide to become less structured or to change the format in some way. The danger is in equating structure with spirituality or form with substance. As culture changes there is also the danger of alienating the next generation, who inevitably have a different view about form and pattern.

As has been stated, a different structure or change will not in and of itself produce worship. Some change takes place because there is no worship. As the world changes, there must be godly wisdom so that how things are done does not supersede why they are done. The "why" is that the Lord Jesus is lifted up in worship and the person of the Father is honoured.

What Worship Involves

Worship is by its very nature reflective; that is, it starts in the mind and involves thoughts about Christ. There are no baskets of first fruits or bottles of perfume that are brought to the Lord, but rather Scriptures, ideas, and thoughts. For the men, these need to be worked out into verbal expressions that lead God's people into worshipful thoughts regarding the Lord Jesus.

With reflection as part of worship, there ought to be some time to gather thoughts and focus on the matter at hand. Whether prior to coming together or as the Lord's people gather there must be some quiet for reflection. It is difficult for many people to go from talking about the events of the week to changing focus to the Lord. In some places, there is little time to collect thoughts before the meeting starts. A solution for some may involve getting up sooner and arriving before the time the meeting is to start.

Many people find it difficult to stay focused, as the mind so easily wanders. The solution has been suggested that if you do not want your mind to wander on Sunday, control your thoughts the rest of the week. Also the thoughts filling the mind on Saturday night may have an effect on Sunday worship.

Worship has been added to the Lord's Supper thus part of what takes place involves remembrance of Him. The command the Lord left us is *"Do this in remembrance of Me"*. The act of eating the bread and drinking the cup is the fulfillment of that command. Only those who know Him can remember Him.

To expand remembrance to the time of worship means that there must be thoughts in the mind that can be recalled. Those who belong to Him must have thoughts of Christ before He can be remembered. Worship, by its very nature, must be Christ centered.

Collective worship involves telling God the Father how much we appreciate and adore Him and expressing our love for His beloved Son. A phrase from Joseph's life illustrates what is involved in worship *"go tell my father of all my glory...that you have seen,"* (Gen. 45:13). If there is nothing seen of His glory during the week, there will be nothing to tell the Father when the saints gather to worship.

There should also be a sense of reverence in approaching God and certainly in talking about our Saviour. How reverence is displayed can be very subjective. Many have a form in mind that to them displays reverence. Things like dress, deportment, style and structure are all part of their view of reverence. To some reverence involves the use of formal language and certain phrases from the 1800s.

Reverence is to a large extent an attitude of the heart, though words and actions may display a lack of reverence and respect. How the Persons of the Godhead are addressed can display reverence or a lack of it. Perhaps a more common issue is a sense of undue familiarity, bringing the Lord Jesus down to our level. Language can be used which would rob Him of His essential glories.

It is good to be careful in addressing the Lord Jesus when expressing concepts that have to do with either His humanity or His deity. It is worth noting that, for the most part, it was demon possessed people who addressed Him by His given name, "Jesus". Those who loved and knew Him called Him "teacher," "master," "Lord" and the "Son of God". His favorite title for Himself was the "Son of Man". In the epistles, other than for specific reasons, He is most often called the "Lord Jesus Christ" or "Christ Jesus our Lord".

An Illustration for Worship

Another Old Testament illustration can be drawn from the instructions given to Israel in Exodus 35 in regard to items brought for the construction of the Tabernacle. The passage starts in verse 4 with a command, in a similar way the Lord Jesus has given us a command, *"Do this in remembrance of Me"*. The response is limited to those whose heart was stirred and whose spirit was willing (v. 21). The Lord is looking for a response from those whose hearts are moved and who want to come and worship Him.

The material that was brought was varied, (vv. 7-9, 22-28), but each item was for a common purpose, the construction of the Tabernacle. All of these items spoke of Christ—each in some way displayed aspects of His Person. No one person brought everything that was needed, but all who brought, presented what they had to give.

So it is in corporate worship. Individuals bring what they have enjoyed about the Lord Jesus. No one person can ever exhaust all there is about any aspect of the glories of His blessed person. Some have greater capacity, and so bring things more precious, but all are needed and valued.

Notice two other thoughts from Exodus 35. One is that all that was brought had come from God in the first place. The people were giving out of what they had taken from the Egyptians, but it was God Who was the source of that wealth. So it is with us today. Anything offered up to God has first come to us from His hand.

Second, notice that all of the materials brought were worked into the Tabernacle by the superintending work of the Holy Spirit (v. 31). The Spirit took all those things and, through men, made the items acceptable as to the finished product. So it is with our worship. It is brought by individuals, but offered up and made acceptable by the Holy Spirit.

Intelligent Worship

A common mistake, usually by younger believers, is to address the Father in prayer and to thank Him for dying for us. There is often in prayer a blurring and merging of the roles between the Father and the Son that indicates either nervousness or a lack of perception.

There are times and places where even more mature brethren will share from the Word or in prayer thoughts that are outside the realm of worship. Sometimes the participation in the worship meeting is used as a "platform" for exhortation, or even evangelism. Some believers have "hobby-horses", and use the liberty of the corporate time of worship to "ride their horse".

There are brethren who are vocal, and will share a passage and perhaps comment without any sense of the purpose of the meeting. In fact, there are some in this category who are "regular as clock work" in their participation, but they end up sidetracking the worship with their lack of discernment. Sometimes it might be in prayer where the same subjects, phrases, and concepts are expressed each week.

The purpose of public expressions, whether in prayer or from the Word should be to direct the thoughts of the saints upward. Stories and experiences can so easily move thinking in a lateral, man-ward direction instead of upward. All brethren should ask this question before public participation: "What will the believers be thinking about when I am finished?"

Will it be thoughts of how clever you are? Will it be the story or experience you shared? Or will the saints think more of Christ and respond with an "amen" and worship from their heart that ascends on high? Will God be glorified and attention given to the Father and His beloved Son?

The Leading of the Spirit

One often hears of the Holy Spirit's leading in worship. This phrase and concept may mean different things to various people. To some it means that the meeting follows a theme—that is, one aspect of the work or Person of Christ is the focus of the meeting. It may be nice to have thoughts and a flow on one topic or aspect but nowhere is this concept substantiated in Scripture.

To others, the leading of the Spirit is seen when a certain form is followed. Perhaps it may be that there is movement in the ideas expressed, progressively moving toward the cross. Some may see leading when the time structure is followed when certain things happen at the proper place in the meeting.

The Holy Spirit leads in life and directs the believer's walk. So the more important aspect of the Spirit's leading in life is day by day. The Holy Spirit speaks to us of Christ, bringing to mind the things the Lord Jesus has said and done. The work of the Holy Spirit in worship is done all through the week, revealing

Christ to us through His Word. There is no switch that is to be turned on when the time of worship arrives so that the Holy Spirit takes over and controls our thoughts and words. If the Spirit's leading has not been experienced in the week, the lack of His leading will be evident in a time of worship.

Worship Through Song

For many in the broader Christian world, there is likely little concept of what constitutes a true worship hymn. Conversely, there are many, especially in assemblies, who would be surprised to find that there are songs of worship outside of a certain hymnbook. "Praise songs and choruses" may or may not contain thoughts that go beyond praise and thanksgiving. Not all songs of worship were written prior to 1950 and are found in only one or two hymn books.

There are hymns written for all kinds of occasions: some for a prayer meeting and others for a gospel meeting. Some are praise strictly for what the Lord has done for us. There are others that are hymns of worship in that they are taken up with Christ. In many hymns, that would be viewed as gospel or praise, there are thoughts of worship that would exalt the person of Christ and bring glory to God.

Sometimes the hymns given out by a brother may be usually sung in a different setting than the worship meeting. Upon examining the words, there may be in the hymn the expression of appreciation of Christ that has stirred the brother's heart. There are modern songs and choruses that also lift up the person and Name of Christ.

Even in the "standard books" that are used there are phrases and imagery that belong to a more literate time. Some hymns are greatly loved both as to the tune and lyrics, but there may be words in them that would not be understood by many. A vocabulary sample from the *Believers Hymn Book* might serve as an example. Words such as "homage", "indelible", "joyful lays", "travail", "recompense", "rife", and "dark vale", are perhaps familiar to those raised with them but unknown to those on the outside. The imagery may also be strange to those who have not been raised in a "meeting". It is difficult to worship intelligently without knowing what is being expressed.

One practical suggestion with regard to hymns and the hymn book is for people to become more familiar with the hymn book. Time can be taken to meditate on some of the hymns and to memorize them so that there can be spiritual songs and hymns in the heart. In this way it is possible to learn and to evaluate the hymns as to their appropriateness for corporate worship.

Consider, by way of specific example, number 447 in the *Believers Hymn Book*, "Teach me Thy way, O Lord, teach me Thy way". This is a lovely hymn, but it is to do with a believer's walk with the Lord. Another such example can be found in hymn number 415, *Master Speak*, which has as its focus the Lord's Word to us and for us.

There are similar examples in *Hymns of Worship and Remembrance*. Number 311, *God moves in a Mysterious Way*, is a great hymn of the faith. Its focus, however, is on His dealings with us in the circumstances of life. Another with similar thoughts would be number 314, *He Leadeth Me*.

These are wonderful hymns, but the direction of the words is man-ward. These hymns have a different emphasis than ones such as, *Lamb of God! Our Souls Adore Thee*, or *O My Saviour, Glorified*. The focus in these hymns is upward or God-ward and the content directs thoughts in that direction.

Verbal Expressions of Worship

The focus on worship means that some items need to be left to another time or meeting. It is not the place to pray for the lost or the sick, as good as this might be, nor is it the time to uphold missionaries and their efforts or even to pray for the outreach of the assembly. The focus is to be horizontal and not vertical.

In older established assemblies, one may hear words and phrases that are repeated over the years. On the basis of constant use these are assumed to be biblical and theologically sound—so much so, that the use is never questioned. Some brethren who would be particular about form and structure may find themselves using such words and phrases, thus expressing concepts that are not true.

A common example can be found in Zechariah 13:6: *"'What are these wounds in your hands?' Then he will answer, 'Those wounds with which I was wounded in the house of my friends'"*. This has often been applied to the Lord Jesus because He had wounds in His hands. He was not, however wounded in the house of His friends, but was hated without a cause. The context of Zechariah 13:1-6 has to do with false prophets, who in their worship of idols have wounded themselves. When they are accused of being involved in idolatry they claim to be farmers and lie, saying that they received those marks on their hands in the home of a friend.

Another example can be taken from Psalm 129:3, *"The plowers plowed on my back; they made their furrows long"*. The context refers to Israel. Verse 1 says, *"Let Israel now say,"* and then the Psalm goes on to describe victory over those who hate Zion. In this context, the Lord Jesus is not in view though it is true His back was beaten.

One more example can be drawn from Lamentations 1:12, the great expression of sorrow that Jeremiah penned. In this chapter, Jeremiah uses a figure of speech called personification. The city of Jerusalem is given personality and words to speak. It is the city that cries out to all who pass by, and asks them to *"Behold and see if there is any sorrow like unto my sorrow..."* It is true the Lord Jesus experienced a sorrow beyond all others. It should be made clear that the interpretation belongs to the city of Jerusalem, and the application is by way of illustration.

There are other expressions used without thought of the implications or perhaps the accuracy of the words. Brethren will talk of the Lord Jesus "making atonement for our sins". Atonement is an Old Testament concept, in that the word means "to cover", whereas the Lord Jesus has removed our sins, washing them away by His blood.

Sometimes both in hymnology and in verbal expressions God is said to be "reconciled". This is a concept which is never found in Scripture. God does the reconciling; it is a divine work whereby God through Christ made it possible for man to come into a relationship with God.

It is good to exercise charity in these things when young men make a mistake in terminology. Many men over the years have been totally discouraged by a rebuke and correction that has left them embarrassed. In such cases it is difficult to ever undo the damage and have these men again take a public part. Godly wisdom must be applied to build up and encourage in such cases so the scars are not lifelong.

Worship is the occupation of heaven, but it should also be the goal of every Christian here and now. The next chapter will explore the importance of worship both for a believer and for a local church.

O God our Father, we would come to Thee,
In virtue of our Saviour's precious blood.
All distance gone, our souls by grace set free,
We worship Thee our Father and our God.

We would, O God, present before Thy face
The fragrant Name of Thy beloved Son;
By faith, we view Him in that holy place,
Which by His dying, He for us has won.

We share Thy joy in Him who sitteth there.
Our hearts delight in Thy delight in Him.
Chiefest of thousands, fairer than the fair.
His glory naught can tarnish, naught can dim.

We bow in worship now before Thy throne,
By faith the Object of Thy love would see.
Who in the midst, His brethren's song doth lead,
To Him our Saviour, shall the glory be.

W. B. Dick

chapter five

THE PRIORITY OF WORSHIP

Worship, as A. P. Gibbs said in the title of his book on the subject, is the Believer's Highest Occupation. The general tenor of Scripture supports this statement. The people that God called and commissioned, such as Isaiah and Ezekiel, are shown worshipping at the start of their ministry. Many of the notable characters of the Old Testament are seen prostrate, worshiping God. In the Psalms, worship is a focal point of religious life and the verbal expression of the nation's relationship with God.

Specifically in John 4, the Lord Jesus tells us that the Father is seeking worshipers. The Lord Jesus came to seek and save the lost, but the Father is looking for worshipers. This is all that the Scriptures have to say about what the Father seeks, which elevates worship to the highest place. It is hard to imagine that the God of the universe, the self-sufficient One, is seeking people like you and me to worship Him!

In the book of Revelation the occupation of heaven is worship: worship of the One who sits on the throne and of the Lamb. There are five "songs" of worship in Revelation 4 & 5. Upon examination the number of voices increases from four living creatures in the first of these, to the entire universe in the fifth. The third is the only true song in that it is sung, the others are spoken. It is a new song—the song of the redeemed who respond to the Lamb and proclaim His worthiness. Ultimately, as seen in the fourth and fifth "songs", the entire universe and every created being will bow in worship. It is at that time that every knee will bow before the Lord Jesus and confess Him as Lord to the glory of God.

In Revelation 14:7 those from every tribe and nation that come out of the Tribulation period are told to, *"Fear God and give glory to Him, for the hour of His judgment has come; and worship Him who made heaven and earth, the sea and springs of water"*. In this current age it is our privilege to worship Him and to give Him glory.

Some believers elevate service to the highest place, and view worship as an act of service. The primary purpose of all things and all that believers might do is to be for the glory of God. When service flows from worship, it puts the heart right with God, and also puts God first.

The first question in the Westminster Shorter Catechism asks, "What is the chief end of man?" The answer given is, "Man's chief end is to glorify God and to enjoy Him forever". All glory will be given to God, and in His presence, there is fullness of joy and pleasure forevermore.

An Illustration

I am indebted to the late J. Boyd Nicholson for thoughts on Ezekiel 44. I have thoroughly enjoyed these over the years. This scene highlights the priority of worship over service. Ezekiel 44 has the prophetic outline of priestly service during the Millennial Kingdom. It is the account of two groups of priests, a particular group of Levites, and, secondly the descendants of Zadok.

The passage starts with God's condemnation of the nation, (vv. 3-9), because they failed to preserve the integrity and holiness of the temple. God says His house and holy things were defiled because foreigners and uncircumcised were allowed to keep charge of the sanctuary.

The Levites in this passage (v. 10), are those who went astray with the children of Israel during days of idolatry. God says of them that they *"shall bear their iniquity"*. This thought is reiterated in verse 12 where God gives His oath as He puts them under judgment. There are consequences for their actions that will limit their future involvement in the work of God. Those limitations are enumerated in verses 11 to 14.

This group of priests is restored to their office, but they are limited to service. They can be involved in offerings and sacrifices for the people but they are excluded from higher privileges.

They cannot go near the holy things, nor can they go into the *"most holy place"*. These priests are also prohibited from coming near God to minister to Him. Though they are restored to service, they were to have charge of the temple for all that is done in it; but there are severe limitations to their sphere of activity.

The sons of Zadok are in a different category as it is specifically said of them that they fulfilled their responsibilities and kept charge of the sanctuary during the times of idolatry. As a result, these priests are commended, and given an expanded role in the temple service. They were to come before God and minister to Him, to offer to God the fat and the blood from the sacrifices. They also get the privilege of approaching the Table and ministering to Him, and having greater responsibility in the work of God.

The lesson from this illustration is that there are two spheres of involvement in the work of God. The first group of priests was to minister to the people of God and be involved in the house of God. The sons of Zadok were to minister to the person of God, things touching the very heart of God.

The ministry to the Person of God and the heart of God was to be done in the intimacy of fellowship with Him. It involved His table, His charge, and an offering of those things that speak of Christ, His person and work. The fat speaks of the inner energy and perfection of Christ; blood speaks of the sacrifice of and satisfaction found in Christ.

These priests had privileges, but they also had responsibilities as to how they approached and entered the inner court. The list of requirements speaks of holiness and purity. The clothing they had to wear was to be white—all linen so as not to cause perspiration. The application is that there is nothing of the flesh but only His righteousness. All the other requirements have to do with not being defiled and hence disqualified from this ministry.

The point of the illustration is to highlight the higher privilege of worship. As needful as ministry is to the people of God and the house of God there is something more. The prerequisites are greater but the privileges are higher as well. To come to the very presence of God, to minister to His person and His heart is a wonderful and lofty privilege afforded those who are holy and undefiled.

Corporate Worship

A phrase sometimes heard, especially so in assemblies, is "the priesthood of all believers". This is most often used to describe the activity of the saints at the Lord's Supper and in worship. Sometime, the priestly activity and function is thought to be exclusive to believers who gather in a certain type of local church.

First and foremost the expressions used by Peter in 1 Peter 2:5, "a holy priesthood," and 2:9 "a royal priesthood," have to do with the believer's position. The phrases cannot be separated from the surrounding words used to describe Christians. So all believers, regardless of how they gather, are "living stones," "a chosen generation," and are "a holy nation," and "His own special people".

The designation of "priesthood" is collective and is used of a group, and does not refer to an individual. The result is that all believers are collectively a holy and a royal priesthood. Darby renders the phrase in Revelation 1:6 and 5:10 "kings and priests" as a "kingdom of priests". James Allen in his comment on this passage says, "while priestly functions are exercised by all believers now in our worship (Heb. 13:15; 1 Pet. 2:5; Rom. 12:2; Phil. 2:17), the word 'priest' is not used in the Gospels or epistles to describe believers". He goes on to describe priestly function as set out in the book of Revelation. "Its use in this book (see also 5:10 and 20:6) makes it clear that the public exercise of such a function belongs to the kingdom in manifestation".

The position of a holy and royal priesthood is demonstrated practically when believers gather and offer up worship and show forth in witness. Collectively this involves giving glory to God and the gospel to man. For this to be true believers must gather to display a priesthood, there is no thought of individual priests. Believers who do not gather with other believers are still part of this priesthood as to their position but in practice they deny its truth.

The Priority of Worship

There is another indication of corporate worship in Philippians 3:3. The context has to do with the contrast between the Judaizers and the believers. In this verse, Paul uses the pronoun "we" to speak of the position that believers occupy. In contrast to the Judaizers who mutilated the flesh, believers are circumcised where it counts—in the heart. Due to this, Christians are able to worship God in the Spirit. A. T. Robertson suggests that this verse should read, "We worship by the Spirit of God." Our boast is in Christ, as opposed to in the law, and there is no dependence on the flesh.

This is true of all believers positionally, again, regardless of how or where they meet. What is not true of all, are these activities worked out in practice. Christians must gather to worship and proclaim the glories of Christ. Where there is legalism, there will be confidence in the flesh and its ability to live a life that pleases God. This confidence will undermine the ability to worship by the Spirit of God.

Individual Responsibility

It is likely that most believers do not understand or appreciate the importance of corporate worship. This is obvious even in assemblies, where the worship meeting is not as well attended in most places as the next meeting, whatever title may be given to it. There was a time when most believers would be at the "Lord's Supper" if they were limited for some reason to one meeting per week.

Corporate worship is not accomplished by sitting in a service and being preached to. It is possible that a congregation, or at least individuals, may worship during the singing of some of the hymns and choruses; form does not dictate substance. What is usually missing is the extended focus that is exclusively on the Person of Christ and the lifting of Him and His Name to the Father.

Collective worship can take place only to the extent that individuals worship. The group does not worship, so there is individual responsibility. This is true in every aspect of assembly life, in that, the assembly functions only when individuals function. Phrases like this are often heard: "our assembly is having an outreach," or, "our assembly has a children's work". These things are only going to happen if individuals are involved. So it is with worship. Believers gather but worship is dependent on individuals. In the Christian life, there are going to be those who prefer to let others "do it". This is true no matter what "it" may be, and holds true in worship. If I as an individual do not come prepared the result will be felt in the time of corporate worship.

It is easy to sit back and complain about issues in an assembly, such as, the worship meeting and how it flows or the lack of worship. It is important in all of assembly life to ask the question, "Am I part of the problem or part of the solution?" In worship, one believer who is truly enjoying the Lord and is excited about His person can certainly have an impact on others.

The time of corporate worship has in most assemblies become part of the "breaking of bread" meeting. In spite of this arrangement the warnings in 1 Corinthians 11:27-32 apply specifically to the act of "remembering the Lord." These warnings are addressed to individuals; *let a man examine himself and so let him eat of that bread and drink of that cup*" (v. 28).

The assembly's responsibility in discipline is outlined in 1 Corinthians 5. The assembly is to gather to deal with a brother or sister involved in sin and who is unrepentant. Such a one is to be put out for discipline, so that Satan can deal with them.

Here in 1 Corinthians 11 it is individuals who have been asked to come and remember the Lord at His command. The warning to these individuals is very solemn: not to eat the bread and drink the cup in an unworthy manner, which would display a lack of discernment. Such attitudes and actions would lead to discipline from the Lord.

In Matthew 5:23-24, another individual responsibility is to get things right with an offended brother before bringing your gift to the altar. How many people over the years have failed to heed this teaching? Many have come to worship when things are not right either with a fellow saint or with his/her spouse.

There are those who are tyrants at home or in the assembly, but who are vocal in worship week after week.

In spite of those warnings and a particular assembly's stand on reception, no policy can stop an individual believer from worshiping. If people sit back or are asked to pass on the bread and cup, they can still sing the hymns and mean what they are singing. They can say "amen" to worship that is offered and can silently lift up thoughts of the Lord Jesus. This point illustrates that worship can and does take place in other formats, and not exclusively in a certain group of local churches.

Conclusion

Worship is to be the supreme goal in the Christian life, both for individuals and local assemblies. It is the occupation of heaven and of those whose hearts are fixed on that place, or more so, on the person of Christ. Every local church should aim to be worship-centered; all activities should start with and flow from worship.

Individually, believers will worship only to the extent that worship is the priority of their lives. It is occupation with Christ out of a heart that is in love with Him that will produce worship. No assembly can solve or resolve a lack of worship without people having a love for their Saviour that motivates them to spend time with Him.

> Occupied with Thee, Lord Jesus, in Thy grace;
>   All Thy ways and thoughts about me only trace
> Deeper stories of the glories of Thy grace.
>   Taken up with Thee, Lord Jesus, I would be;
> Finding joy and satisfaction all in Thee!
> Thou the nearest and the dearest unto me.

C. A. Wellesley

chapter six

THE PRODUCTION OF WORSHIP

The worship meeting in most assemblies follows a certain form. There is an opening hymn or a word of welcome or a Scripture read and perhaps a few comments. Depending on the local assembly there is likely a progression of hymns, prayers and in many places verses are read. All of this precedes the breaking of the bread and drinking of the cup, which usually come near the end of the meeting. The general idea is that there is a progression of thought that climaxes with the breaking of the bread.

There may be variations at the start or end of the meeting. Some assemblies would open the Word and have comments or teaching only after the emblems are passed. However, in all of the arrangements, there is not a single word from Scripture as to format or procedure. That fact does not stop many people from having strong opinions on these things.

There are groups of assemblies in various parts of the world that would make some of these the reason to be in fellowship with other assemblies. If there were to be any variation from the pattern, it is likely fellowship would cease between what had once been similar assemblies.

Not to belabor the point made earlier, but, it becomes so easy to elevate how things are done above why and what. Ritual takes precedence over reality and the fear of man over the fear of God. The autonomy of the local assembly is denied in practice, and men are elevated to headship in the church. In such atmospheres, how can real worship take place from the heart?

It is relatively easy to become proud, to be puffed up because of perception, principles, privileges or practices. It has been said that people can be proud of, "race, face, place and grace". It is good to remember that God resists the proud and gives grace to the humble.

Form is not totally immaterial and structure does lend itself to certain types of response from people. So having a dedicated time of worship associated with the Lord's Supper has great value. The danger is equating form with substance and being proud of the light one has and thinking others do not have the same light.

An Illustration

Another illustration I heard from J. Boyd Nicholson, taken from the Song of Solomon 5:2-5, is worth repeating here. In her dream the woman is in her chamber when her beloved knocks on the door. She does not answer right away because she has just got into bed. In the following verses (vv. 6-8), she goes out into the streets to find her beloved, but is found by the watchmen and beaten by them.

The point of the illustration is that in the first part she was in the right place, but her heart was not right. In the second part of the story she is in the wrong place, but her heart is right as she seeks her beloved. The question that flows from this is, "Which is the most pleasing to the Lord?" That is, to be in the right position but in the wrong condition, or, to be in the right condition but in the wrong position. The answer is that neither pleases the Lord, but His desire is that His people would be in the right position and in the right condition.

The application is that doing things as to procedure may put you in the right position, but without a heart full of Christ the condition is wrong. What is needed is for both position and condition to be in place.

Conclusion

There are good things happening in a number of local assemblies around North America with many keen young people. There are youth and young families, excited about the things of the Lord and anxious to honour Him at home and in the local church. There is evidence in many places of young men being in the Word and enjoying the Lord.

There are also alarming signs in some places. There are assemblies in numerical decline, with few young people, and limited prospects for growth. There are some assemblies that are moving away from a dedicated time of worship, which is certainly their prerogative. What is being lost is a sense of worship as the believer's highest priority.

Fewer homes have libraries with good reading material; there is a lack of good books and Christian magazines visible. Experientially, there is a noticeable decline in conversation about the Lord Jesus and His preciousness. There is no lack of talk, but much of it is horizontal and less and less vertical.

The solution to all of the shortcomings and deficiencies can be found in the love we have for Him. The person, who knows that he/she is forgiven much, loves much. Those who love much will want to spend time at the Lord's Table learning from their blessed Saviour. Worship will flow from this time spent with Him. May our prayer be, "More love to Thee, O Christ, more love to Thee".

More love to Thee, O Christ, more love to Thee!
Hear Thou the prayer I make on bended knee.
This is my earnest plea:
More love, O Christ to Thee. More love lo Thee.

Once earthly joy I craved, sought peace and rest.
Now Thee alone I seek, give what is best.
This all my prayer shall be:
more love, O Christ, to Thee. More love to Thee.

E. P. Prentiss

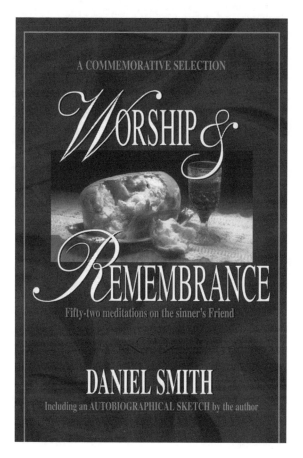

A COMMEMORATIVE SELECTION

Worship &

Remembrance

Fifty-two meditations on the sinner's Friend

DANIEL SMITH

Including an AUTOBIOGRAPHICAL SKETCH by the author

Worship and Remembrance

by: Daniel Smith

The highest occupation of the human mind, the sweetest ministry of the human heart, is the worship of God and the remembrance of is Son. It is the only passion to which we may give ourselves without reserve, with no fear of being corrupted by it. We will never be reprimanded by Heaven for exaggerating the Saviour's worth!

But what is worship? And what is it we are to remember about Him? This volume is filled with "sweet incense" to offer up to the Lord. The Scriptures are full of Christ, and this book is full of the Scriptures.